Take This Walk
With Me

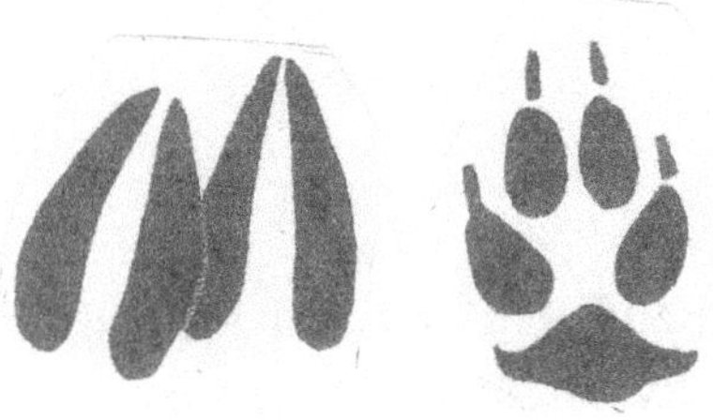

Dr. Barbara Callison

with music by

Susanne Mulcahy

Printed in the United States of America
by CreateSpace

ISBN 978-0-692-01727-2

Cover Photo by Judy Kramer

Cover Photo of Tony Kramer and children

Acknowledgements

Many thanks to my husband, Paul Anderson, and Vandy Shrader for their suggestions and editing of this book. I also want to thank Judy Kramer for the cover photo and her valuable help with its production.

I wish to express by gratitude to Susanne Mulcahy for her beautiful guitar music that inspired the title for this book.

Lastly, I could not have written this book without the teaching, support and advice of the Environmental Volunteers.

****

Other Books by Barbara Callison

Humphrey The Whale Who Lost His Way   1987

Growing Up In Los Altos   1992

Swim for Life   1998

INTRODUCTION

This book is intended to encourage parents and adults to take children outdoors for meaningful walks through different environments to discover relationships in nature. These days, it is more important than ever before to get kids outside. Why?

Today's children spend less time connecting with the natural world around them, than they did even twenty years ago. The reasons are varied; some of these include: the increased demands on kids' time from homework, music lessons, and organized sports; the amount of time they spend sitting indoors, interacting with technological gadgets; and the concerns parents have about the safety of allowing their kids to play outside. Schools are not providing as many field trips as they once did due to lack of money or lack of adult supervision as more parents work full- time. While the way humans interact with nature has changed in the last generation, what has not changed in the last twenty years is nature with all its interconnections.

As a result of societal changes, kids today are missing the joy of exploration in the great outdoors, a curiosity about nature, a love of the outdoors that includes an awareness of connections humans share with plants and animals, and a sense of responsibility for the health of this planet.

My own love of the outdoors came from my parents who were backpackers and fly fisher persons. We spent vacations traversing the Sierra Nevada mountains in California. Since I did not like to fish and was an only child, I amused myself through exploration. Little did I know how valuable those experiences would become later in life.

In addition to having a career as a scientist, I have been a docent for almost thirty years with an organization called the Environmental Volunteers (EVs). They are based in California at the EcoCenter in the Palo Alto Baylands. The objective of the EV's staff and volunteers is to teach natural science to elementary and middle school children, through classroom activities, field trips, and summer programs. The EV strives to promote understanding of and responsibility for the environment through hands-on science education and positive interactions with nature. For more information about the Environmental Volunteers, please visit their website: www.EVols.org.

A song written by Susanne Mulcahy, a past director of the Environmental Volunteers, inspired the title for this book. In 1998, she wrote, *Take This Walk With Me,* as background music for a video of the same name that the EVs were putting together. If you would enjoy hearing this song, it can be downloaded at the following URL: www.EVols.org/song

By leading children on field trips, and using my own experiences, I have been able to view first-hand the benefits of connecting children to different environments.

In this book, you'll learn about the many benefits of spending time outside, you'll learn how to make an outdoor excursion fun, and you'll discover new ways to explore and understand the natural world that surrounds all of us. My hope is that you will use the information and suggestions in this book to become an effective leader to your children, getting them off the sofa, out the door, and into nature; and in the process help them to develop a love for nature and a desire to take care of Earth.

GETTING STARTED

If you as a parent have not spent a lot of time outdoors, it may be difficult to know how to get started. Keep in mind that getting outside is the ultimate goal; don't let the details stop you from getting out the door.

Discovery and Curiosity. A nature walk should encourage discovery and inspire curiosity. Discovery is a great teaching tool. In order to get the most out of the discovery process, leave the Ipods, phones and headphones at home. People using these devices while walking, running and biking are missing the ability to experience the wonderful sounds and sights of nature. In addition, nature provides a quiet place to get away from the noisy, rushed world many of us experience today.

Here is a suggestion for easing yourself into the natural world. Walk slowly in silence for a few minutes or sit if you prefer. Experience the sounds, smells, sights and textures of nature. Notice the rustling of birds in the brush. Breathe in the fragrant scent of a bay tree growing nearby. Be dazzled by the vibrant colors of the beautiful wildflowers blooming near the trail. Run your fingers along the rough surface of an oak trunk.

After the period of silence ask yourself some questions, beginning with: "What did I hear, smell, see and feel?" Allow your answers to lead your thoughts down new pathways. Did you hear birds singing or chirping? What message were they conveying? Did you look at the clouds? Why are they shaped that way? Who or what made those holes in the ground? How did the animal dig the hole?

We can learn a lot about interacting with the natural world

by observing young children. Pre-school children, especially, have a natural curiosity about their surroundings. Take a small child on a walk and watch how they notice ants or other insects on the ground. Sure, their eyes are closer to the ground than those of adults, but they also have an innate desire to stop, observe, and ask questions. Young children have no fear of getting the "wrong" answer. They know that in nature there are no wrong answers, only the desire to know more. The more they know, the more kids want to know. The advantage to increased curiosity about nature is that it leads to increased knowledge.

What's in a name? If you're concerned that you won't know the name of what you are observing, don't let that stop you! Adults have been conditioned to believe that it is necessary to know the name of everything, but that's not true. Discovery and curiosity are more important to exploration, than knowing the name of everything.

Questions and guesses. The same can be said about questions and answers. The need to know the answer to a question is instilled in adults, but guessing is better. Guessing makes one think; the answer can always be found later on the Internet or in a book. Looking up answers together is a valuable project for parents and children. Encourage children to guess at answers to questions, and let them see you make guesses.

Even when you are asking questions, keep talking to a minimum as kids tune out long discussions. It's more important to listen to their answers. See where their interests lie and steer them in that direction. The outing will be more fun for everyone if this advice is followed.

The way questions are asked is important. When you ask, "What do you think?" there is no right or wrong answer. Many school age children have been conditioned to come up with the right answer but this method can stifle curiosity. Try not to ask yes or no questions but leave the questions open-ended for increased thinking. Questions such as, "What name do you think we should give this animal or plant?" are designed to encourage children to use their imagination. Or you could say, "Why are these creatures living here?" (*it is moist, and dark,*). "What do you think they eat?" (*minerals from the tree*). Later in this book is a list of sample questions to make children think.

Where to go. Now that you're ready to explore, you'll need to choose a suitable location. Personal exploration is an important part of any learning experience. Meaningful explorations require a kid-friendly environment. When choosing an area for personal explorations, keep the following suggestions in mind:

- Don't select a strenuous walk or one that is hot and dry. Comfortable walks are best.
- Pick an area with lots of trees, as more animals or evidence of animals will be present to explore. If a creek, lake or pond is nearby, that also adds to the variety of plants and animals to be found.
- An easy way to get involved with nature is to participate in the many clean-up days offered by cities and states. There are beach clean ups and river and creek clean ups. Or you may want to volunteer to clear trails and pick up trash. This is a good way to instill values that we as humans are responsible for the health of earth.

EXPLORATION ACTIVITIES

Now that you've chosen a location for your outing, you'll need to have some fun activities to keep your children engaged. The following ideas are intended as guidelines.

Establish a sense of connection with a place. When I'm leading a group of children on a hike, I like to start off by sharing my feelings about the area; why I love this place. When I discuss what this area means to me, I am communicating a love and respect for the land. Many times I share what I did as a child in the outdoors. I talk about the beauty and majesty of a redwood tree or the special qualities of a particular animal that lives in the area.

What animal are you? Sometimes, I'll ask children what animal they would like to be and why. I tell them that I would like to be an otter, because I love the water and otters always appear to be having fun.

It's a mystery. If children complain about going on a walk, make a mystery out of the experience. Ask, "What do you think we are going to see?" You can follow up with questions like "Where do you think we'll see that?" or, "How many do you think we'll see?"

The alphabet game. Have kids find letters of the alphabet in nature. The tree below has a Y and a V. The two mushrooms could be B or an eight. You could also have them find nature objects that start with alphabet letters. For instance, B is for banana slug, and O is for oak tree.

Counting fun. You could give your kids a job to do such as counting the number of trees or the number of banana slugs they see. Each time a child encounters another of his or her item, you could share another fact about it, or you could have the child tell *you* something about the animal or plant.

Colors in nature. Have a collection of paint chips in different colors of plants or animals you think might be found in nature. (You can get free paint chips at any paint store.) Let each child pick a color. Their task is to find a plant or animal that matches their color. Then talk about what they found. Ask questions such as, "Why do you think it is growing in this spot (*sun, shade, temperature, soil type*)?" "Why is it that color? (*photosynthesis*, attract *pollinators, camouflage*)"; "Does it have a smell? (*protection from insects or to attract pollinator*s)."

Anybody home? Encourage them turn over rocks or logs to see what is underneath. Say, "Let's see how many things we can find under this log," or, "What do you think we'll find under this rock?" Bring an inexpensive magnifying glass along to look for spiders or their webs, or other small animals such as sowbugs or roly-polys, earwigs, ants, termites, worms and even fungi. These animals are called **the recycling squad** because they digest dead logs, leaves and even dead animals, and return the nutrients to the soil. Without these valuable *recyclers*, the forest would be clogged with dead branches and logs. Observe and count these organisms that make their living as *decomposers*.

Who eats whom? See if your kids can figure out who eats whom in the natural world, starting with plants, then moving to plant eaters *(herbivores)*, meat eaters (*carnivores*) and meat-and-plant-eaters (*omnivores*). Have them create different food chains beginning with the same plant. Or, introduce them to the concept of a *food web* by pointing out all the different food options for each member of the chain.

Food Chain

Using your 4 senses. Give children time to use four of their senses: allow them to see, touch, smell, and hear, but not taste, items in nature. You might ask them, "What do you hear?" or "What does this smell like?" or "Describe what this feels like."

Animals at work. Children who observe animals at work gain a deeper understanding of what animals do. Take time to watch ants at work. Ask questions such as, "Where are they going?" or "How do they know where to go?" "Do they go alone or in groups?" What do they eat?" "How are they connected to humans?"

Tracks. Kids love finding and following tracks. If you

want to see good tracks, go out after it has rained, as tracks will leave deeper impressions in damp ground. If a creek is nearby, animals will have traveled in the area for water. If you find tracks, ask your kids, "Who do you think made those tracks in the mud?" You could ask, "How many animals were there?" "What direction were they going?" "Do you think it was a large or small animal?" Have them look closely at the details of the tracks. Ask, "Does the track show claws or no claws?" "How many toes does the animal have?" Bring along a track book to figure out which animal belongs to the track.

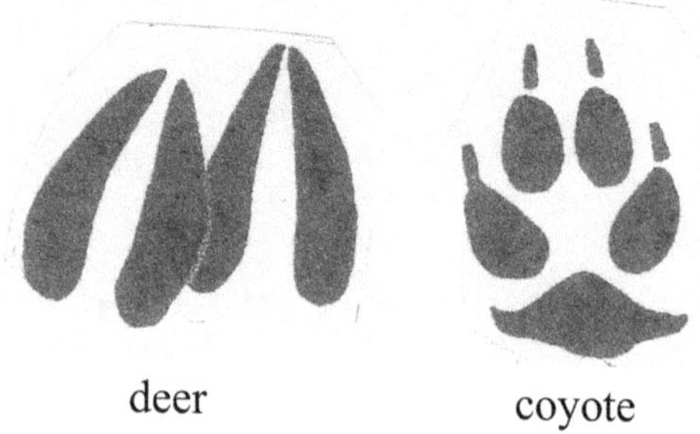

deer   coyote

Here are instructions for making track impressions:

1. Buy plaster of Paris in a hardware store
2. Put a cup of plaster in a metal can and mix in enough water to make it moist but not soupy.
3. Place a cardboard ring around the track to contain the plaster.
4. Pour the plaster over the track (about an inch deep is plenty).
5. Allow the plaster to dry for 1/2 to 1 hour, then remove the cardboard ring, dry and lift the plaster.

The animal's track should be imprinted in the plaster.

Brush off the dirt, and wash the dried plaster if necessary. I've done this for young children and the track has become a cherished possession.

Pattern discovery. The natural world has many patterns that we can discover when we take the time to look closely at the things around us. Kids love to look for and find patterns. During your walk, take some time to look for patterns displayed in the natural world. Below are some well-known patterns found in nature.

- **Spider webs.** Have children look at different spider webs, and look for the patterns within them. You could ask, "Do all spiders build webs the same way?" or "How is this web different from that web over there?"

- **Snails**. Which way do the shells turn – to the right or left? Do all shells turn the same way?

- **Leaves.** Leaves have many different shapes, vein patterns, and growth patterns.

- For instance, some leaves grow opposite from each other on a stem, some grow in a spiral pattern, and others grow in clumps. Have children examine different types of leaves to find the vein and growth patterns. Make sure you know what poison oak, poison ivy and stinging

nettles look like as these plants can cause skin
irritation when touched.

    The golden mean. One interesting pattern found
in nature is called the *golden mean* (that's *mean* as
in *average*, not *mean* as in *unfriendly*). The
golden mean is a ratio that the Greeks recognized
through repeated observations of natural objects.
The golden mean can be found in many different
places in nature: examples include the ratio of an
insect's three body parts to each other, the length
of our hand to our forearm, the sizes of the
decorations on a peacock's feather, and the sizes
of flower petals. It also underlies the pattern found
in the whorls of a pinecone, or the spiral of a snail
shell.

Mathematically, the golden mean describes a ratio of parts
as shown below:

A--B---------------------------------C

If you compare the length of the small segment line BC, to
the length of the larger segment AB, you get a ratio of
1:1.618. If you then compare the length of the larger
segment AB to the whole line AC, you get the *same* ratio,
1:1.618. These segments can then be said to adhere to the
golden mean.

Look at the picture of the
ant. Note that the ant's
body has 3 distinct
segments, the head, thorax
and abdomen. If you were
to compare the length of

11

the ant's abdomen to its thorax, you would get a ratio of 1.618; similarly, if you were to compare the length of the ant's thorax to its head, you would get a ratio of 1.618.

You can apply the same reasoning to the three parts of some flowers or the three parts of a peacock feather.

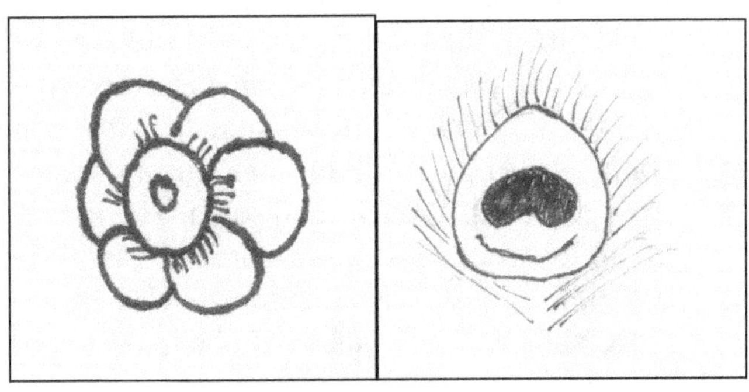

•

Nature abounds with examples of the golden mean! See if you can find some of these ratios through observation, then let children try to see this phenomenon in nature.

WHAT NATURE CAN TEACH US

Connections. One of the important concepts to introduce to children is that everything in the natural world is connected to something else. John Muir stated, " When one tugs at a single thing in nature, he finds it attached to the rest of the world."

    Who? Many of the nature activities suggested above can be used to explain the concept of connections in nature. For instance, in the "Who eats whom?" nature activity, the child learns how

12

all the members of a *food chain* in nature are connected to everything else. You can expand the lesson in many directions. For example: The backbone of the food chain is plant life. Any animal that eats primarily plants is called an *herbivore.* Think of all the animals that depend on some type of plant life for their nutrition: rabbits, deer, snails, fish, ducks and so on. The list could go on forever. Going a step further, ask, "Who eats the animals I just mentioned?" Hawks, wolves, birds, and seals would be good responses. These animals are *carnivores* or meat eaters. Animals such as raccoons and bears eat both plants and meat and are called *omnivores.*

From here, you can go in many different directions. You could ask, "Are you an omnivore?" or "Who are the top predators in this area?" It is good to use terminology such as *herbivore* and *predator* as you are reinforcing what children are taught in school. You might also ask, "What happens if we remove one part of the food chain?" Let your children's age and interest level determine the direction of your questions.

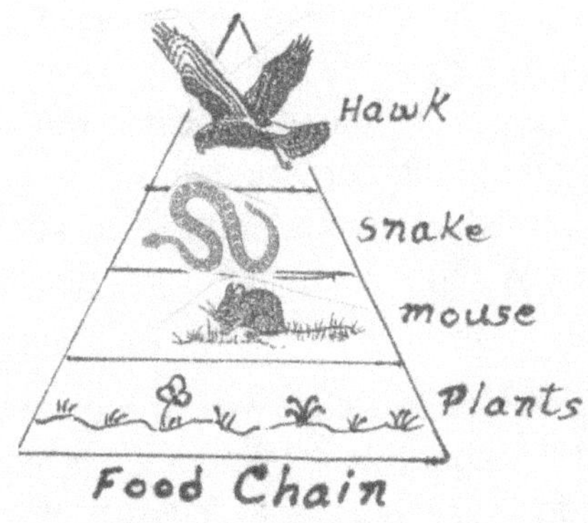

⚔ **Where?** Another type of connection concerns the area where you are walking. You could ask, "What if this forest were cut down for a shopping center or a parking lot?" Let children think of the possibilities that may occur after the project is completed. Their answers (and your follow-up questions) will depend in large part on the ages of the children. Answers may include the possibility that several animal habitats will be destroyed, or that insects living under the bark that provide food for other animals will be gone. Then you could ask, "Will they go elsewhere?" (*They'll have no choice*.) or "Will the climate be changed?" (*Yes, if the area is large enough. The sun's rays will now be able to warm an area that was once cool. Less oxygen will be released into the atmosphere by photosynthesis due to fewer trees.*)

You could also ask, "Will erosion occur?" (*Definitely yes, if the trees are growing on a sloped hill,*) followed by, "Is this good or bad?" (*Bad; if enough top soil is eroded, as it has a bad effect downstream for other areas.*) According to the book *Collapse,* by Jeremy Rifkin, past populations in places such as Easter Island disappeared due to over-cutting of trees and other plants for wood, building and farming. In turn, this action led to erosion and loss of good topsoil for planting crops. Without adequate crops, people starved or succumbed to disease.

    The basics. Another way to look at connections is to think about the basic items all living things need to survive: *Sun* for energy, *Water* to grow and transport materials, *Wind* for transportation and cooling, and *Soil* for nutrients. A good question to ask is, "Are they all equally important?" Follow up with, "What would happen if water disappeared?" (*Plant and animal cells would shrink and cease to function. The organism would die.*) "What would happen if the sun disappeared?" (*With the sun's energy and warmth gone, photosynthesis would cease; many organisms would die from decreased temperatures.*) "What if the wind stopped blowing?" (*climate would be affected; some seeds would not get dispersed*) "What if the soil went away?" (*food production for plants, animals and humans would be decreased.*)

You can choose to explore these connections further. For instance, if you followed the *soil* connection, you could ask, "Why is soil important?" (*Animals and plants use soil as a source of nutrients and as a habitat.*) You could tell them, "No matter where people live there is soil on the ground." You could ask, "Where did the soil come from?" (*It's made up of small pieces of larger rocks that have broken down, evolving slowly from surrounding rock material, taking longer than our lifetime*) and have them look for the mountains or streams that might have brought rocks to this area. You could also ask, "Why are soils different colors and textures even within the same area?" (*They are made from rocks of different colors and types. Since there are many different kinds of rocks, there will be many different kinds of soils. Factors such as water, erosion, plant life and weather further alter soils.*)

Stewardship.

Children who spend time in nature develop a feeling of closeness with the land, which often translates into a desire to care for the environment, to be its steward. There are many ways to help children learn to care for Earth. Below are a few examples to get you thinking.

- **We are guests here.** To provide a sense of stewardship for the land during your nature explorations, emphasize to children that this area (forest, field, beach, swamp, etc.) is the home or habitat of many animals and plants, and we are the guests. Ask your children, "How can we be good guests?" Some answers could include: "After we have looked under a log, we must gently replace the log to its original position" or "We need to be sure to pack out any trash we bring in, or pick up trash we find along our walk."

⋏ **Don't pick me!** Once leaves or flowers are picked they are lost forever. Emphasize to children that they may smell or touch leaves, bark, or flowers, but they should not pick them. The plant needs their leaves, bark or flowers much more than we do!

⋏ **Touch me gently, and then put me back!** It's natural for children to want to pick up objects. With adult supervision it's okay to gently pick up an insect, banana slug, or other harmless creature, as long as the animal is replaced—gently—to its habitat. Remind children that objects such as rocks, sticks, and acorns can be picked up and observed but not removed from the area, as animals or plants may depend on these objects for survival.

In these small ways you are providing children with a sense of caring for the natural world, teaching them to become stewards of Earth.

THE MANY BENEFITS OF SPENDING TIME IN NATURE

There are so many benefits to being outdoors. Nature promotes a healthy lifestyle that curbs obesity, promotes brain relaxation, piques curiosity, increases science test scores and provides an understanding of ones' role in our universe.

It's also free! An afternoon spent at a local park, vacant lot or schoolyard doesn't cost anything, yet provides bountiful benefits. Even if you have to spend a little bit of money to visit a state park, it costs much less than the latest app, video game or other technological gadgets that encourage children to sit indoors in their free time. If you're interested in learning more about the natural history of urban spaces, a good book to read on this subject is *Vacant Lots* by Matt Vessel. Keep reading to learn about more of the benefits from spending time in nature.

Intellectual benefits: A Classroom in the Woods. Outdoor experiences enhance the learning process and lead to increased science literacy.

With the use of today's PET scans and MRI technology, it is possible to show how the brain is shaped through experiences. Stimulation in the form of hands-on personal explorations and exercise results in several physical changes in the brain. One change is the growth of new extensions called dendrites on neurons (brain cells).

Neuron

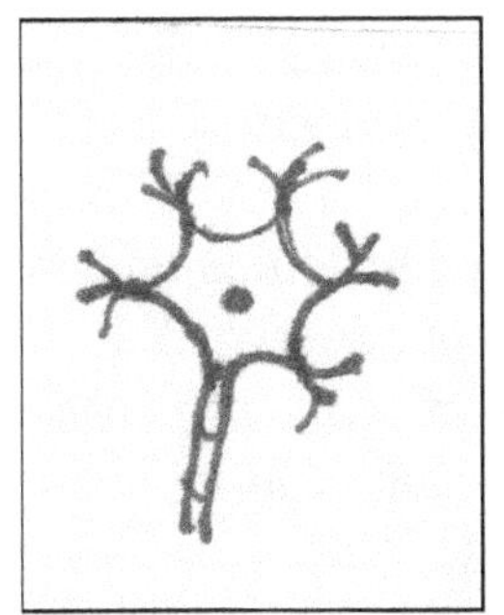

The more dendrites a neuron has, the faster it can communicate with other nerve cells. Another change is an increase in the number of receptors along nerve pathways transmitting information to the brain, allowing more and faster connections. When nerve pathways are stimulated repeatedly by new experiences, the brain stores this information and learning has occurred. Today the scientific community agrees that intelligence is a function of experience. Emotional experiences also affect brain function. Anxiety stimulates body glands to release chemicals that may inhibit learning. Being outdoors can be a calm, soothing experience for children. Having fun and being outdoors encourages the release of chemicals that inform and regulate new information to the brain for enhanced learning.

The Environmental Volunteers have performed assessment studies on their method of using trained volunteers to teach natural science activities in the classroom followed by leading these same children on field trips to further stimulate curiosity and personal exploration. Each year these students receive a new topic. Brain pathways are stimulated in the same manner for several years in a row, ensuring retention and new learning. Results in schools where all grade levels received the EV's instruction have shown an increase in science literacy on test scores.

Physical and psychological benefits. Spending time in nature is also good for the body and spirit.

> **Sleep.** It is well documented that sleep helps the brain and body restore itself. According to the National Wildlife Federation's (NWF) new parent guidebook, *Green Time For Sleep Time*, by Kevin Doyle, busy schedules, television watching and playing with electronic devices are depriving children of precious sleep time. Sleep deprivation can stunt growth, impede performance at school, lead to depression and contribute to health problems. Elementary school age children should sleep at least ten hours per night to perform well the next day. Spending time outdoors helps to regulate the body's internal clock in the brain so that children and adults are alert during the day and tired at night. Concentration improves with

more sleep and as more time is spent outdoors.

Depression and ADD (attention deficit disorder). Today, more children are diagnosed with either depression or ADD today, than they were 50 years ago. Is this due to better diagnostic tools or are children exposed to other factors at home and at school? The answer is probably both. Decreased sleep and a lack of exercise can be underlying factors in both depression and ADD as shown in studies in *Medicine & Science in Sports & Exercise.* When you don't get enough sleep, depression and ADD symptoms will be worse. Children and adults become grouchy and the ability to focus decreases.

Exercise is one of many treatments used for depression and ADD. Earlier, I discussed how increased blood flow releases chemicals in the brain to encourage more brain cell connections for better learning. There are also feel-good chemicals released that change mood. It has been proven that depression can be reduced by exposure to light. The best source of light is outdoors. Light stimulates an area of the brain to release mood-altering chemicals that are capable of modifying depression.

Children with ADD are hyperactive and may lack the ability to concentrate. These factors make it difficult for them to learn in a classroom situation. Being outdoors provides a calm, serene environment in which concentration may be improved. Walking, hiking, and running increase blood flow to the brain, which can improve focusing ability for a sharper mind. Exercise also reduces excess energy to promote a better night's sleep.

⚘ **Stress.** When I was growing up, I did not know the word *stress*. I was too busy playing outside at school and at home. Today, I hear elementary school-age children discuss how stressed out they feel. Light to moderate stress can benefit body functions while severe, long-term stress may be harmful. Excessive amounts of cortical hormones and adrenaline are primarily the culprits for harmful stress. One suggestion by the medical profession to relieve stress is to participate in an exercise program as it rapidly clears the body of these hormones. Children use recess at school to stretch out body muscles, ease tension, and clear the brain. Physical activity during recess uses up the harmful hormones that have been released during the day due to anxiety.

Big changes in schools occur when less money, curriculum demands and testing impact school time. Recess gets cut back and less time is spent outdoors. It is more important now for parents to ensure children are outdoors after school and on weekends. Children still need to clear out the hormones, especially if they have had a tense, anxious day. Get them to take a break from the electronic toys and go outside to play.

Stress and lack of sleep can also reduce the efficiency of the body's immune system. This is the

system responsible for protecting the body from the
invasion of bacteria and viruses. Upper respiratory
infections (colds) are reduced in people who
exercise on a regular basis. Exercise appears to
stimulate blood flow, and increase production of
blood cells and chemicals involved in the germ
fighting process. Nature provides a quiet respite
from the hectic, rush, rush world we live in today.

Obesity. Sufficient research exists on this subject
to convince educators, doctors and parents that
there are an increasing number of overweight
children. Any exercise is beneficial, by
encouraging a change in lifestyle. Spending time
in nature will provide exercise as well as the feel-
good chemicals that come with it. Short bouts of
exercise will lower triglyceride (fat) blood levels
as these molecules are used to provide glucose for
necessary energy. But the exercise must be
performed daily, weekly, and monthly to have a
permanent change in body weight. Even moderate
obesity poses risks to overall health; it is
implicated in diabetes, cardiovascular disease,
pulmonary disease, certain cancers, and
gallbladder disease. It takes time for these risks to
appear. Children should start early to develop
positive exercise habits to avoid problems later in
life.

Spiritual benefits. People who spend time
communicating with nature see everything with a
new pair of eyes. They have a better understanding
of their place in the Universe, and their relationship

to the stars, plants, and animals. They understand the interconnectedness between everything on this planet, and their importance as a link in that interconnectedness.

Understanding this interdependence can be difficult, as we don't live long enough to experience all the relationships that are occurring, or that have already occurred. We didn't experience the beginning of Earth or the solar system so how do we know what really happened? I had an eye-opening experience about fifteen years ago, when I had the opportunity to travel on a small raft down the Colorado River through the Grand Canyon for two weeks. As I traveled deeper through canyon walls, I could look up and observe two million years of rock that had been laid down before I was born. I felt so small in comparison to what had occurred before me and would occur again after I am gone. I can only imagine that men and women who travel in space and look back at Earth feel the same way.

VALUES FOR TODAY AND TOMORROW

We all develop values about the world around us. I am convinced that our values about nature are developed from our early family experiences first, followed by school experiences. Children learn value systems at a young age by watching, listening and participating with other children,parents, and teachers. These people become role models for children's attitudes. Adults, especially parents, become the most important of these role models; as a result of this, adults should care about the values they pass on to children.

Educators agree that value systems are developed at an early age. If so, then children need to start early spending time outdoors to develop values that encourage a respect for and an understanding of open spaces. Think about how you spend your weekends. Do you go for a hike or bike ride? Do you encourage your children to play outside after school or during vacation? Your children are learning how to interact with the world, through you.

Understanding the relationship between nature and humans sets up value systems used to make important environmental decisions throughout life. There are many issues before us today that involve nature. Just look at topics in newspapers, magazines, on the Internet or on television. A few that come to mind are coastal protection; safer, cleaner bays and oceans; adequate, clean water supplies; energy sources; pollution; preservation of animal habitats; and global climate. Many issues require voter decisions. Who are our present and future voters? We make the choices on issues today, but our children are the future voters. How are they going to make wise decisions on environmental issues if they don't understand, value or love nature around them? As John Muir said, "To love something you must experience it first."

QUESTIONS THAT STIMULATE THINKING

The following questions may be useful to stimulate curiosity and connect children to the environment. Feel free to adapt the question to your situation. You may also come up with some of your own.

- ⅄ Feel some leaves and then ask, "Why are some leaves hard and waxy while others are soft and fuzzy?" (*Waxy leaves conserve water and deter insects while fuzzy leaves are usually found in shady areas.*)

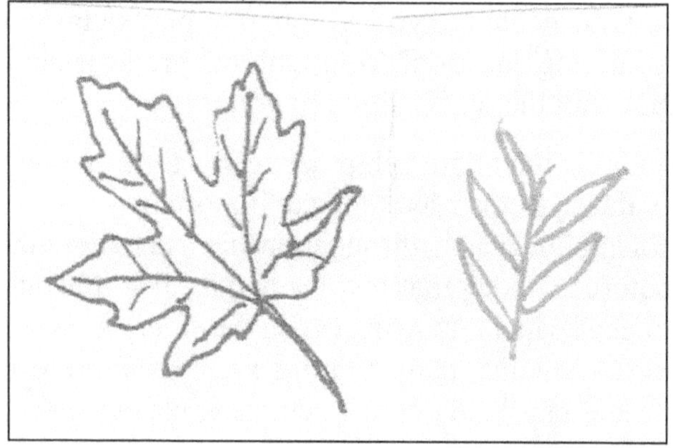

- ⅄ "Why do leaves come in different sizes and shapes?" (*Small leaves conserve water loss and are usually found in hot areas, while large leaves on a plant are in shady, damp areas.*)

- ⅄ Observe birds in the sky or on the ground. Then ask, "Why do some birds fly in big groups while others fly alone? Is there an advantage to either way?" *(Big groups provide protection.)*

- ⅄ In the spring, observe the variety of color within flowers. Smell different flowers. Ask: "Why are flowers different colors and shapes?" or "Why do they bloom at different times throughout the year?" *(A flower's purpose is to reproduce by attracting pollinators – bees see different colors and scents than a hummingbird or an insect sees. Shape allows pollinators access to the pollen.)*

⅄ Observe holes in the ground. Ask, "Who made that hole and why?" or "What did they use to dig with?" *(Children often answer that snakes made the hole—ask them to think about how the snake would have dug the hole.)*

⅄ Observe different colors of dirt. Ask, "Why is dirt different colors?" *(Different minerals in the rocks provide different colors plus varying amounts of dead materia*l.) or "Where does soil come from?" *(Hills with streams that carry small rocks.)*

⅄ "What parts of a plant are used by squirrels, birds, and insects?" *(Fruit, nuts, leaves, seeds, sticks, branches, bark.)*

⅄ "What does an animal's track tell us?" *(It tells us the kind of animal, its size, and the direction it is going.*)

⅄ "Which of the following can smell: worm, sowbug or any fungi?" *(Fungi cannot smell.)*

⅄ "Do you think spiders can smell?" (*Yes, using hairs on their leg*s) or "How do they see?" (*With up to eight compound eyes.)*

⚶ "How do ants talk or communicate with each other?" *(Using smell-chemicals and body language.)*

⚶ "Why do ants communicate with each other?" (*To indicate a food source, to aid with reproduction, to make nest markers, to make an alarm signa*l.)

⚶ "How is this plant or animal adapted to living here in this dry, rocky (or other) area?" *(In hot environments, animals live underground and plants have small, oily leaves; rocky areas provide shade and safe habita*t.)

⚶ "How many different ways are seeds dispersed?" *(Wind, water, animals, fire.)*

⚶ "What does scat (poop) tell us?" (*Fur in the scat tells us an animal was consumed and this scat belongs to a predator such as a coyote, fox, or bobcat; seeds or a dark color tell us berries or fruit was consumed; small round droppings may belong to a rabbit or deer.)*

⚶ "Name some animals that we cannot expect to see in the daytime, as they are nocturnal." *(Mountain lion, raccoon, skunk, owl, bat, etc.)*

⚶ "Can you name animals in this area that hibernate during the winter months?" *(Snakes, tortoise, etc.)*

⅄ Pick up a feather on the ground. Ask, "Who does it belong to?" If you have water with you, place a drop or two on the feather. Ask, "What happens to the water and why?" *(If the feather is fresh, the water should roll off as birds put oil on feathers from oil glands to waterproof them.)* You can identify the bird feather using the following URL: The Feather Atlas

http://www.lab.fws.gov/fa/idtool.php?button

⅄ Compare eye location on a coyote versus a deer. Ask, "Why is there a difference?" *(Coyote's eyes in front provide depth perception that is needed for a predator, while a deer needs eyes on the side of the head for wider vision, as they are prey for larger animals.)*

⅄ "What are the different ways birds are communicating with each other?" *(Singing a song, chirping, repeating a call, etc.)*

⅄ "If you are in a redwood forest, how are you connected to the redwood tree?" *(They provide oxygen, store carbon, and provide shade, climate control, and wood for firewood and for building.)*

⅄ "If you are in an oak woodland area, are the

connections the same?" *(Oaks provide a food source with acorns while redwoods do not.)*

OPEN-ENDED QUESTIONS

These questions will start discussions that may expand well beyond the original question. Remember, there are no wrong answers.

- In what ways might the environment be affected if this forest is cut down?
- Who will be affected if a shopping center is built on an empty lot?
- Make up a food chain for the area where you are right now.
- How are recyclers or decomposers important in nature?
- What good things do plants do for us?
- How are you connected to this area?
- Who will be affected if a dam is built on a river?
- Do birds matter? If a pesticide killed all the birds in this forest how would nature be affected?

CONCLUSION

The focus of this book is *to get children outdoors to observe, to explore, to be curious, and to ask questions, **all while having fun!*** It's not important to know the name of everything; you can guess or make up names for things in nature. It *is* important to nurture and encourage children's natural curiosity and their innate connection with nature. Ask questions that get them thinking, and then let their answers guide you along the path of their interest.

You parents can enhance your child's learning by providing more time outdoors. Get to know what curriculum your kids are studying in school, and follow up on science topics with an outdoor trip.

By incorporating the ideas and activities presented here into your outdoor excursions, you will help children increase their science knowledge, improve their physical and psychological well- being and develop a greater sense of responsibility for the care of this planet. You now have a powerful tool for increased learning.

My vision is that all children be so inspired by the natural world that they will want to spend time outdoors learning more about plants and animals. In doing so, they will develop a caring attitude for the preservation of these resources. And they will develop a desire to become future stewards of the land.

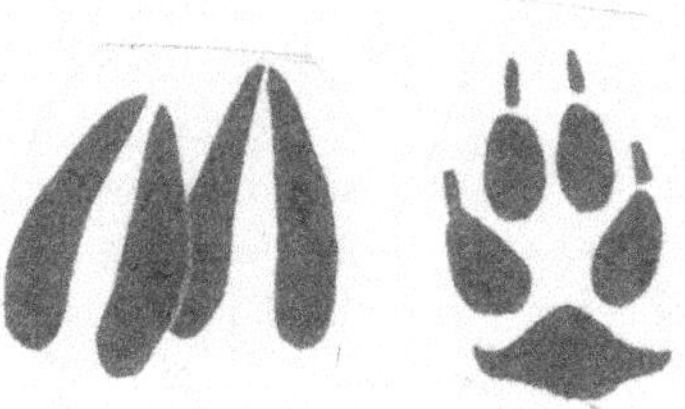

GLOSSARY

Consumer	an organism that eats prey
Carnivore	an animal that eats other animals
Decomposer	organisms that cause the decline of organic material
Diurnal	active during the day
Food chain	the transfer of food energy through various species
Habitat	the living place of animals
Herbivore	an animal that eats plants
Hibernate	to spend the winter in a resting or sleeping state
Nocturnal	active at night
Omnivore	an animal that eats either plants or other animals
Photosynthesis	how plants make glucose
Pollination	transfer of pollen
Predator	animal that preys on other animals for food
Prey	an animal taken by a predator

About the Author:

Barbara grew up in Los Altos, California in the 40's when it was orchards and open fields that presented opportunities for exploration with nature. Today, Barbara has a doctorate in science curriculum and instruction and taught for 25 years at San Jose State University, first in the Natural Science Department and later in the Geology Department. At the same time she taught an anatomy and physiology course at De Anza Community College.

Since retirement in 2001 her first love has been the outdoors where she leads field trips for adults and children. She also teaches natural science in the local elementary schools as a volunteer for the organization, Environmental Volunteers (EVs) based in Palo Alto, CA.

About the Musician:

Composing since she was 12, Susanne is a singer-songwriter in the folk tradition with a passion for harmony. Her music reflects a deep connection with the earth and nature, and the sacredness of life and relationship. She is known for her powerful voice, engaging delivery, and connection with the audience. Susanne is a 1998 San Jose Film and Video Commission Joey Awards Original Score Finalist for "Take This Walk With Me," the title song and soundtrack to the instructional video which she co-wrote and co-produced for the Environmental Volunteers, where she served as Executive Director from 1994-2000.

Susanne has performed throughout the San Francisco Bay Area at festivals, community events, private celebrations and rituals. Currently, she is a member of the Global Heart Choir and the music ministry team at the Center for Spiritual Living, San Jose.

Proceeds from book sales to be donated to the EVs.

ISBN 978-0-692-01727-2   US $9.99